C000001924

Guide

*In olden days a glimpse
of stocking was looked
on as something shocking
but now Anything Goes*

By David Johnson and Roger Dunkley
Drawings and design by Julia Stone
Photographs by Bob Baker

· OLD HOUSE ·

Contents

Photographs

Published by Old House Books & Maps,
PO Box 883, Oxford, OX1 9PL, UK
1385 Broadway, 5th Floor, New York, NY 10018, USA
www.oldhousebooks.co.uk

Old House Books & Maps is part of Bloomsbury Publishing Plc

© 2013 Old House.

Transferred to digital print on demand 2016

First published 2013
2nd impression 2013

Printed and bound by PrintOnDemand-Worldwide.com, Peterborough, UK

A CIP catalogue record for this book is available from the British Library.

ISBN-13: 978 1 90840 256 1

Originally published in 1967 by Atlas Publishing, London.

Gear Gets Going

London as the centre of the swinging, with-it, hip—or whatever vogue word is currently popular with the journalists—fashion world, is now generally accepted. There have been articles about it in *Time* magazine, in all the foreign press and on most countries' television and film screens. There is even a complete LP record, 'London Swings' by the Jack Johnson Orchestra. The leading symbols of the scene are the mini-skirt for women and very brightly coloured gear for men. We aim to tell you something about the beginnings of this fashion take-over by London, how it swung into top gear, where to go in London to find the shops and boutiques which sell gear—and where you'll see a large number of people wearing the latest clothes.

Since starting—nearly ten years ago—it has spread rapidly and now there are boutiques in all parts of London as well as some great ones in most other English cities. We have not attempted to cover all these in the directory because some of them sprout and go like mushrooms. We have concentrated on those areas in London where the scene started and where it is strongest today. The two districts which saw the beginnings of the new scene are still the most important, Carnaby Street, Soho, and King's Road, Chelsea.

Late in the 1950s London first became aware of something new happening in the fashion world. Paris has traditionally been the centre for new fashions and they have been worn by the wealthy—and usually older—members of society. London has always had a name for good suits and materials but nobody would have pretended that new clothes ideas were born there. Suddenly two things happened: new materials and revolutionary fashions were appearing and they were being worn by the younger set. Designers had always looked for new ideas year after year and new materials but in the past they were always variations on a theme—long skirts one year, shorter the next; narrow shoulders, wider shoulders; stripes now, checks next. It was always within a fairly narrow range of variations that clothes altered and it was aimed at a small group of people—the relatively rich, older group.

Pop Leaders

It was the young who brought London to the fashion world's attention, nearly a decade ago, by wearing bright colours, new materials which were not necessarily expensive and generally altering the look and ideas of clothes both for boys and girls. Why did the young cause this change—some have even called it a revolution —and what were the groups of people behind the new movement? The answer is that in Britain young people were starting to have money and influence. Leaders of this world were the pop groups, supported by young photographers, designers and a whole host of youthful successes. John Michael—one of the leaders of the new fashion mood, said: 'The desire was always there, the need to dress up and be smart but it was dormant. The war years had made everything so dull and the English-man's image had become one of dowdy conformity. I began a few years ago and for some reason people have been copying me ever since. We introduce a new fashion—like the colour purple for men, the striped shirt or denim and within a few months every other shop in London is marketing a copy. That's when we know we have to drop it and search around for something else . . .'

The young people had money to spend and saw the new fashion ideas on beat and pop groups on television and in the press and suddenly they were all taking a new interest in clothes. Not only the girls. The boys as well were keen to wear bright, gay clothes in materials not used before and so powerful has the whole movement been that it spread right through the community. You can buy pink suits for men now in Carnaby Street and three tone shoes—modelled maybe on racing cyclists' footgear—probably older men won't go wearing this sort of gear but the effect has spread. You'll probably see bright ties and coloured coats now, even at boardroom level. The young still lead but they've dragged everyone else along with them.

Carnaby Clicks

Carnaby Street is still the real home of this great movement. The fact that it started there is really pure chance. One man who played an important part in the early stages was Bill 'Vince' Green, a young photographer with a business in Newburgh Street in London. Vince was a stage portrait photographer who specialised in taking shots of body-builders. One of his problems was finding briefs that were brief enough and close fitting to show off the body beautiful to the best effect. There seemed to be no solution to his problem until Vince started making the briefs himself. He tried using stretch materials intended for women's roll-ons and other unlikely cloths. It was really only a part time activity for Vince, but his name spread—people started turning up and asking for briefs to order in unusual materials. Even visiting royalty sought him out and were fitted with swimwear. In 1954 he visited Paris and was struck by the clothes of the beat Left Bank student fraternity and café society—young people who lived it up through the night in the cafés wearing dark glasses and a lot of denim.

Denim took Vince Green's fancy. He discovered that people were actually bleaching their denims and sitting in baths to shrink them to body hugging shapes. It seemed a great idea and Vince decided to sell denims made like this. In October 1954 he opened up a boutique selling pre-shrunk, pre-bleached clothes. At the beginning the trade was highly amused and thought it a quickly passing gimmick. But soon he was supplying his denims wholesale to big stores like Harrods. Today, over a decade later, this particular gear style is still very popular in many different forms. It's not surprising and new as Vince probably thought. In the days of the great army of the Russian Czars the officers were known to sit in hot baths to soak their sealskin trousers body tight before a big parade or ball.

Bouncing Boutiques

Vince's was probably the first boutique. It was quickly known to the new money earning young who were prepared to spend plenty of their earnings on looking good. Enough of them went to his place to ensure the success of his new venture.

But it was the next move that probably had the greatest effect on really getting the gear scene moving. An assistant to Vince—John Stephen—moved away and worked in a number of other small clothes shops specialising in new look clothes in the Notting Hill and Baker Street district of London. These new little shops, bright, gay and intimate (unlike the traditional big clothes store or specialised shirt or men's shop) proved to be very successful. Stephen decided to set up on his own. He came back to Soho, the area where Vince had started, and opened a one room boutique on a second floor in Beak Street which is round the corner from

Carnaby Street. These were quiet little streets with a mixture of old shops and firms in them and one of the reasons he chose that area, was that being unfashionable, the sites were quite cheap. Despite the area, Stephen's little shop did well until going out to lunch one day, he left the electric fire on, some curtains were blown on to it and by the time he returned his stock was blazing merrily. That would have been the end according to Stephen, had it not been for a very sympathetic landlord who happened to have an empty shop round the corner in Carnaby Street. This was early in 1957 and the street was anything but swinging—just a line of rather dowdy small shop fronts. Stephen got going however, painted up his shop in bright gay colours which made it stand out like a fun palace and promptly started doing well.

A little later in 1957 Andreas Spyropoulos, a small shirt manufacturer from north west London who had found the only way to compete with the big boys was to produce designs and materials that were different, was offered a property in Carnaby Street but turned it down because he reckoned it a dead area. Stephen's success showed that it was possible to do well there with new fashion ideas and in September of that year Spyropoulos changed his mind, took one of the cheap shops and started what was to become a very successful line of boutiques called DONIS.

Pop Patronage

By 1962 Carnaby Street had really boomed and was beginning to look like it does now. That was the year of the first Beatles record and the decline of some older idols from the top of the hit parade. With the appearance and influence of the new groups who used clothes to put over their new image, boutiques became big news. The Groups were very influential and many of them took to appearing on television and at shows in different gear for every performance. The accent was on novelty and change. Clothes which were bright, different but quite often inexpensive—after all they might only be worn for a few weeks—began to spread. Many of the leading Groups sought out Carnaby Street with its new ideas and talked about it in public. As pop music became a bigger influence so did the with it clothes worn by the Groups.

Boutiques really started to sprout in London, bringing with them a variety of new clothes ideas. They all had certain things in common. They were small, brightly coloured, intimate and completely unlike the traditional places for selling clothes. They changed their decor and designs often and tried to find as many original ideas as possible. The fact that they change as the fashions change has made people say that they won't last, that the whole scene is a passing one which will be just a myth in a few years. This seems unlikely. Though clothes may now be bought and worn for only a few months, the boutiques have continued and grown in numbers. Whatever some critics may feel, they'll go on.

Buttons and Bows

After DONIS, other specialist shops started to appear in Carnaby Street. The BUTTON QUEEN—a shop which specialised in buttons of all kinds—moved from West London to a button-sized shop which was formerly a cobblers, just off Carnaby Street, because Toni Frith liked the rather 'village' atmosphere which seemed to be growing up there. George Mallard, who'd been nearby for about ten years, began making swinging cheaper versions of his beautiful model hats and changed his shop's name to HAT GEAR. John Stephen opened a girl's boutique. Steve Topper opened up a show boutique. There were over thirty boutiques in narrow Carnaby Street and John Stephen had nine of them.

The reason for Stephen having nine instead of one big shop was that the intimate atmosphere of a boutique is better suited to with-it clothes than the big formal layout of older shops. Stephen could specialise—selling shirts and ties in one shop, trousers and socks in another—and even where he didn't he found that the small gay boutique with pop music playing was far more attractive to the new young buyer. Carnaby Street began to look like a brightly coloured fair with lines of enticing booths offering choice and excitement. What's more, the customer has direct contact with the designer and the changing trends are easier to display.

Hip Huggers

Andreas Spyropoulos claims to have made his first hip-hugging trousers—hipsters—after he'd watched a large number of his customers pulling his slacks down over their hips—possibly in imitation of Roger Vadim who wore his that way. John Stephen made his first high collar shirts after watching his customers trying to make the shirts they tried on visible above the laps of their jackets. Often a new design would be the result of an experiment or a copy of what some well known figure in the pop or film world had tried out, or even a design accident pounced upon and exploited.

Carnaby Street is a narrow, exciting little road which wouldn't be recognisable now to someone who knew it fifteen years ago. It has a market atmosphere of gaiety—rather different from another London road which has also played a big part in the London fashion scene—King's Road in Chelsea.

King's Swings

King's Road is a more likely place for a new scene in fashion to start. It has always been a street where unusual and interesting people can be found. Some years ago Chelsea was an artist's area. It has now been largely taken over by a mixture of the wealthy young with-it groups and the successful: TV producers, film men, well known writers and models. They jostle in the shops with the younger members of old English families with famous names. Because of the people living in the area, its pubs and entertainments have long attracted lots of others to visit it. It was not surprising that King's Road should also sprout boutiques and shops where new things were happening.

One of the most imaginative and inventive people whose influence has been considerable on the Chelsea scene is Archie McNair who used to run a photographic studio in the King's Road. In the early 1950s McNair opened the FANTASY coffee bar in the King's Road—one of the first when they were newly coming into fashion and a leader in what later became a craze. McNair was friendly with a lot of with-it trend fashion conscious people who found in his business sense and eye for future fashions a means of getting their ideas off the ground. Mary Quant described in her autobiography how her husband, Alexander Plunkett Green and 'the Nair' combined to set her on the business road. And what a road!

This was 1955, it was the beginning of the girls' half of the gear revolution in the clothing scene. Some reckon that Mary Quant with BAZAAR was the very start of the whole swinging world. She was certainly a dynamic early influence. Although Vince started the year before, Quant's impact was more direct and widespread on both the public in general and the world of fashion in particular.

Quantity

The idea that Mary Quant should go into clothes fashions was no more odd to those who knew her than that King's Road should be a scene for trendy shops. Since she was a little girl, she had been designing her own clothes and inventing new ideas for wearing things. She realised that girls were ready for a big change in their approach to clothes just as the boys were. They had money as well and wanted to look gay and exciting. What suited their mothers didn't suit them. They wanted colour and excitement rather than an exclusive model dress. In London visiting, discoteques, jazz clubs, coffee bars and places blossoming they wanted to feel and look good and different. They needed young ideas from young designers. People over thirty were out and not in tune with their needs and mood. Quant was ideal—swinging, pretty and full of ideas herself, she could supply just what was needed. She was the leader for a whole host of young designers with the feel of the age—particularly for women.

In the clothes trade people predicted a short life for Mary Quant. Concentrating on new colours, modern designs and a rapid turnout of clothes went against the old traditions of proved fashion. By all the old rules, they should have been right.

Yet Mary Quant's success was quite spectacular. She was a brilliant young designer and there were plenty of young people anxious to appreciate her talent. Her initial shop was so successful that other boutiques sprang up in the King's Road very quickly—almost overnight. It was in 1957 that John Michael opened the first man's boutique at number 170. He called it SPORTIQUE. John Michael had been a women's fashion designer in his mother's business but going into men's fashions had always been his ambition. Men's clothes had looked pretty sad for over half a century. Yet there had been past times when men had dressed dandily in gay colours and flattering styles. Why not reintroduce such fashions, bringing them up to date and using the latest materials? The first thing to get rid of was the old baggy trouser style and next to reintroduce shoes without laces. He also put colour back into men's clothes. Why shouldn't they wear red trousers, bright ties and gay jackets? He quickly proved that there was no reason at all. He introduced too the idea of matching gear— ensemble wear—with complete outfits designed to harmonise. This was new thinking that hardly matched the traditional foreigner's idea of what sombre, quiet Englishmen wore. But it worked a treat from the start.

Savile Surrenders

The leading designers in the new trends vied and influenced one another. Soon, John Stephen opened up a place in King's Road, while John Michael spread with places in the heart of the traditional tailoring area—Savile Row and Regent Street—as well as shops in Oxford Street and Old Compton Street (another Soho street not far from Carnaby Street). Now both John Michael and Mary Quant have boutiques in Bond Street—traditionally the high fashion area.

Recently the number of boutiques has grown enormously. They are in all parts of London and most other towns and cities. In London the biggest groups are still chiefly in Carnaby Street and other parts of Soho, in King's Road and other parts of Chelsea but they can be found in Hampstead, Ilford, Croydon—in fact anywhere where there are shopping areas and young people to buy. It's interesting to see the big traditional shops joining the trend. They are all opening up little boutiques within their main stores. Woolands (Knightsbridge) were one of the first with their 21 shop, Austin Reed's opened CUE and Selfridges started MISS SELFRIDGE. More and more of these shops within shops are opening up but they lack somehow quite the intimate gaiety and liveliness of the small solo boutiques which is part of their charm. 'One feels almost a fool if one doesn't own a boutique', said Clement Freud the well known journalist recently, and although he was exaggerating, you can see what he meant.

Boutique Fronts

Gear Goes Global

At the Palace Hotel in St. Moritz in 1959 a fashion show had been arranged which included such well known leaders of haute couture as Victor Stiebel, Mattli, John Cavanagh and Worth. Mary Quant attributes the fact that she was included with this list of established fashion figures to the need for some comic relief. Whether this was so or not, the fact remains that she astounded her audience with her new swinging designs. After all the staid ball gowns, mink coats and formal dresses of the traditional designers, there was a sound of jazz and to it a stream of girls appeared wearing short, high waisted flannel-dresses, coloured stockings and knee high boots. No one had seen anything like it and there was an enormous demand for the new designs. The local shops would have bought the whole collection, lock, stock and barrel if it had not been in bond by local customs regulations.

When Mary Quant went to New York soon after with her husband, she again got a rave reception. She had no prior build up, no great publicity gimmicks and no special contacts. She just took two suitcases full of her latest designs which she showed to the *American Women's Wear Daily*. This powerful fashion paper went mad about them. 'English chic is fiercely *now*—by the young for the young. Where did the English chic come from? Well, it's always been there but it's on an added fashion-wave length now.' The chicks were chic!

The American fashion world took to the new with-it looks just as the Continent was doing. *Life* Magazine ran stories about it and *Seventeen*—one of the biggest selling magazines for the young in the States—offered a special spring promotion. Soon after this, Mary Quant was offered a contract by the J. C. Penney Company Inc., the biggest chain of retail stores in North America. She took it and went into mass production for the first time, but it worried her a little. It's not easy to keep the dynamic new look fashion kick up on a mass scale, even she would agree that it's best in the small in-world of the little boutiques. But as she says herself: 'Our decision was influenced by our belief that the whole point of fashion is to make fashionable clothes available to everyone.' So the Ginger Group was launched.

Pop Goes the Bistro

Quant had made a success of her showings first time round in St. Moritz and the States but the acid test was to come in Paris, traditionally the home of fashion leading and haute couture. If she could break through there, she would really have achieved a resounding success. Encouraged by her other successes, she went ahead in really bold style. Against the marble and crystal background of the swish Crillon Hotel she unleashed to the rows of waiting critics and designers . . . polyvinylchloride—PVC! The 'Wet Collections' as they were to be known made an enormous impact and had a resounding success.

The idea of such new fabrics displayed against a background of swinging jazz was quite new to the rows of watchers. What's more the Quant show was conducted at high speed—unlike the old sedate pace of the traditional houses. The idea of using PVC for garments was a real breakthrough. It raised some pretty difficult production problems—it took two years to solve the question of how to make a really satisfactory PVC seam—but the interest aroused that year in Paris by the Quant show using man-made fabrics of all sorts instead of imitation natural materials has continued steadily ever since. Even the squarest of the traditional houses has bowed before the gales and makes use of materials it thought were only intended for aeroplane seats.

PVC has been taken up wholeheartedly by the French and put to enchanting use by designer Michele Rosier. It's been seen in the Paris collections of Balmain and St. Laurent while the latest ideas in fashion design for the space age by such designers as Texan Ruben Torres, can be traced back to Quant's 'Wet Collection' of 1960. Torres said: 'You couldn't make the Empire State Building out of marble, could you? The couture of Paris today is still much of it working in fabrics which are the equivalent of marble.' There is little doubt that Quant had made this point some time earlier.

The new thinking was picked up by the French fashion papers *Elle* and *Jardin des Modes* and repeated in all the English press. Normally the *Sunday Times* Fashion Award goes to one of the well-known traditional couturiers but that particular year it went to King's Road's Mary Quant. She's had a hand in bringing out a lot of other new fashion ideas. As early as 1959 she had anticipated the current French craze for 'culottes' or knicker-bockers, whether worn underneath or without a skirt. She was almost certainly responsible for another gay idea—the fun-fur— showing that it is more amusing and far cheaper, to use ordinary rabbit, maybe dyed in all sorts of new ways, than the classic, staid mink. This attitude is right in keeping with all the other ideas of the gear revolution designers—to make clothes which are fun, cheap, gay and can be changed after a while for something else. The furriers are probably fighting a losing battle against that one so they've joined it.

Paris took up the fun-fur craze and extended it, using brightly coloured fur in strong pinks, oranges and yellows to create devastating further effects.

Le Mini

The one garment in the whole new fashion trend which has received more attention than anything else has been the mini-skirt—maybe because it reveals so much of that much discussed topic, a girl's legs. In the 1920s and early 1930s, England had had the flapper girls whose skirts were thought to be very daringly short. They were nothing compared with the mini-skirt. Started in England, it has caught on in many other countries, but you will still see the shortest, most daring and exciting mini-skirts on the streets and in the boutiques of London. It met some opposition at first. Lovely English mini-skirted model Jean Shrimpton was not well received in sunny Melbourne in 1966 and Moscow and the eastern capitals are slow to take up the trend in a big way but it is away to a great success in New York and Paris and only recently Mary Quant opened up seven boutiques on the Via Margutta in Rome.

The mini-skirt was undoubtedly an English invention. Probably the first were shown by John Bates of Jean Varon and it was Bates who did the design for Diana Rigg's TV series, THE AVENGERS. This programme was certainly influential in spreading the trend and it was a very short time before minis were appearing in all the boutiques. The skirts were made even shorter than the first ones and shown in new swinging way out colours. Paris, as it often does, went one better making an invaluable contribution to the development of the mini-skirt. It designed the 'total look'. Cardin in particular took the mini-skirt and had the idea of adding matching stockings and leg flattering shoes to give an all-over look. The mini-skirt was now well and truly launched. The give and

take on fashion ideas between London and Paris has always existed although it used to be mainly giving by Paris and taking by London. Now the roles had evened out or even reversed. No one would deny that the trouser suit is a French idea. It was first shown just about five years ago by Courreges, but it was in the with-it scene of London that the trouser suit really caught on in a big way. Thousands of girls wore them—not only in the King's Road or Carnaby Street but everywhere—and the mass manufacturers had the courage and imagination to put them in production long before they were common in France.

Men's Gear Fashions Fashions Abroad

British inspired fashions for men have been slower in penetrating abroad. In the States, despite the big articles on London's scene, the more extreme and way out styles for men are still worn by a relative minority, such as students, people in the film and fashion worlds. The average American young man is still pretty conformist compared with his English counter-part and is more likely to go for safe looking clothes of the Ivy League variety. Their trousers have baggy thighs and are usually tapered; jackets are usually three buttoned and single breasted. You are less likely to see on Broadway the flaring bell-bottomed, hip hugging English trousers in bright checks, or gay stripes and double breasted jackets in exotic materials and designs.

However John Stephen has found that he can make inroads in the American fashion world. His debut in the States was in the summer of 1965 when he opened a boutique within a department store called Dayton's in Minneapolis. *Look* Magazine ran a special four-page feature called 'The Minneapolis Mods' all about how the new English styles were going to dominate the American scene. Within a week the entire stock was sold out.

Since then he has opened boutiques **within** department stores in about twenty **cities** scattered right across the country as well as in large cities in Canada. The broad outlines of the new look are becoming accepted and it probably won't be all that long before anything in the new English fashion scene goes. The main features which are catching on are very natural shoulders to coats high waists tight thighs and slightly flared trouser bottoms.

All these features have been incorporated by Pierre Cardin in his men's clothes. In fact it would be true to say that the English look is now more popular on the Continent than at any time since the high old days of the eighteenth century dandies when men like 'Red Herrings' Lord Hertford's illegitimate son founded the French Jockey Club. The English have been known on the Continent for horsy styles more connected with country houses and grand leisurely living in the past but this is all changing. The new colourful English scene is all the rage.

Casual Gear

We have been talking about the more formal side of the gear scene—the complete outfit looks and complete ensembles. But all part of the gear wear are the extras and accoutrements —the jeans and hipsters, the reefer jackets and caps belts and socks. The influences which changed these are less easy to pin down. Some of them started in England, some came from other sources or from unexpected places like the army or sailing gear. Sometimes things seem to go round in circles. George Mallard of HAT GEAR had a buyer from St. Tropez recently who wanted a sailor cap so that he could copy it to sell in his own boutiques. Surprisingly enough, the prototype for the cap had come from the sailing fraternity in St. Tropez about three years before!

There was certainly a craze in France

recently for wearing naval surplus clothing which was being sold off in the markets. It was cheap and it looked good because it was rather rakish. Students started the vogue and it quickly caught on, both for men and women. Lately there has been a great demand in London for old military uniforms of all sorts ranging from the magnificent tunics of the eighteenth and nineteenth centuries right up to the wearing of modern military coats and hats. There are now a number of boutiques which specialise in selling military uniforms and accoutrements of all sorts —places with wonderful names like I WAS LORD KITCHENER'S VALET. Who can say what really got this going ? Possibly the Beatles appearing in one of their films in military regalia. The newly fashion conscious with-it young buyers have realised that the eighteenth century was a great period for colourful exciting dress—even amongst His Majesty's forces.

Another big influence has been the Western. With its tough heroes dressed for work and play in blue denim and leather, it was an obvious style to copy and has been taken up in a big way. First we saw the ordinary blue jeans, but now you can buy in London's boutiques, denim shirts, denim ties, suede overcoats and a whole range of leather and denim clothes which were certainly not worn by the pioneers in the Old West. Some of the first young people in England to wear this sort of gear were the so called 'Mods' of the early sixties who cultivated long hair and rode motor scooters in large groups. They wore brightly coloured denim trousers and ex-army leather jerkins and certainly played a part in the fashion scene.

In fact, the boutiques take fashion ideas from anything that suits them. Articles and films about the space age suggested the idea of space age clothing—using plastics and zips where once it would have been cotton or wool and buttons. Sports quite often give the new designers ideas. Many of the current acces-

sories have been taken from the sailing world with nautical caps and buttonless coats like sailing jackets. Another clever idea which the boutique owners have made much of is to use materials which are well known but not for the particular garment in question. Like, for example, making shirts from paisley tie materials or trousers from materials which would only have been used once for skirts. Ideas may come from the young wearers themselves who suddenly start a fashion—like wearing rugby football jerseys as mini-dresses or adapting old Victorian dresses.

Opinion Overseas

What do other countries think of this sudden fashion leadership by Britain? One French criticism is that the new English styles are badly made and hastily put together. When Peggy Roche, a fashion editor of the smart French magazine *Elle* came to London in 1965 as guest fashion editor of the new magazine *London Life,* she was very eloquent about the excitement of English clothes, both the gear in the boutiques and the ready-to-wear versions. But she bought all her own clothes in France because she maintained that the English do not care about fit, are bad at making good seams and have little idea about matching. Some of this may be justified but the new clothes are made to wear for short periods usually, not to last for years—fashion changes too fast for that, often now from month to month. The important thing is that the new clothes are bright, gay and essentially cheap. In a boutique like BIBA in Kensington or in a range from a mass manufacturer like Samuel Sherman which can usually be found in the boutique chains, you buy the latest fashions long before the more expensive Paris copies are out. Although the French are trying hard to reduce their prices, the cheapest clothes in a good boutique like DOROTHEE BIS in Paris are from Mary Quant.

How To Get There

As we have already mentioned, the two main areas for boutiques are Carnaby Street and King's Road. Other boutiques are scattered in various parts of central and outer London— they are usually bright and gay enough to pick out in a flash. Carnaby Street is on the fringe of Soho, an old London area which is now the heart of the city's clubland and contains many great, foreign restaurants. Soho lies between Shaftesbury Avenue and Oxford Street, so is very central. The street itself is a narrow one which runs parallel to Regent Street and it only takes about five minutes to get from one end to the other. The nearest Underground station is Oxford Circus. From the tube station entrance walk down Argyll Street past the well known London Palladium, turn left at the bottom into Great Marlborough Street and cross to the other side. Just a hundred yards along turn right into Carnaby Street. The area is a meter zone so you'll have some difficulty parking especially on Saturday mornings. There are an enormous number of enormous buses which stop at Oxford Circus but if visiting London and staying in a central hotel, the easiest way to Carnaby Street is to call a cab— any driver will know where you are talking about and it's a short run.

While in the Carnaby Street area don't miss the ten minute walk into the heart of Soho. The Street runs North-South and by turning left at the southern end and walking for about five minutes you will find yourself in Wardour Street,

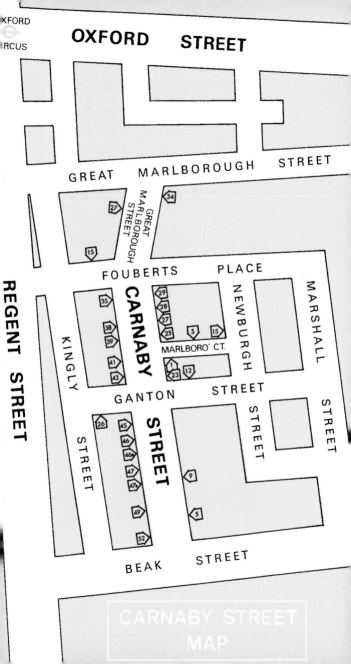

home of the British film industry but well equipped with other boutiques, jazz clubs and coffee bars. Within a quarter mile radius is the most interesting area in London operating deep into the night. Keep your eyes open—you'll see plenty of examples of the gear from the boutiques being worn in the streets—and a lot of home made gear you won't even find in the shops. If you meet a group looking at first sight like eighteenth century Hussars officers, don't wonder whether you've been taken back a couple of hundred years by mistake—it's probably a crowd of young Londoners heading for a night out in one of the clubs or discos.

King's Road is less central than Carnaby Street. It is wider and much longer and runs westward from Sloane Square which is the most convenient Underground station. If planning on visiting the boutiques at the western end of King's Road like GRANNY TAKES A TRIP hop a cab down the road and walk back—that way you'll see the scene without tiring before you've covered the whole road. Buses in plenty go to Sloane Square and several of them run down the King's Road. Again visitors from abroad will find it simplest to take a cheap cab to the area—it's as well known to the drivers as Soho.

The best plan when visiting the King's Road area is to make a day of it. Visit some of the shops and then have lunch in one of the many attractive restaurants along the road. They range from quite cheap to very expensive so you'll find something to suit any pocket. Or go into one of the many pubs where you'll find some pretty good examples of the latest gear being worn. The *Chelsea Potter* and the *Six Bells* on the left hand side or *Finch's* on the right are all pretty swinging 'liquor parlours'. Or if you want to keep it teetotal drop in to the Kenco Coffee Bar—you'll see some exciting gear there and interesting people, if you can see behind the 'shades' they're wearing. King's

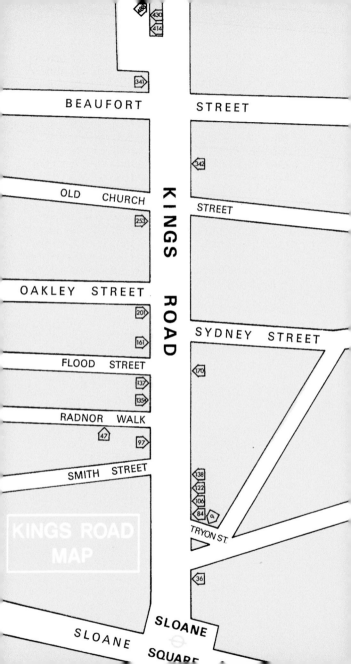

Road deserves a leisurely look because in addition to the boutiques are a large number of other interesting shops including scores of antique dealers. It is easier to park in Chelsea than in Soho, but still pretty crowded. Choose one of the many turnings on the south side of the street (the left hand side approached from Sloane Square)—you'll find yourself in one of the many lovely little Chelsea squares that abound in the area. If you ask the way and choose someone wearing military gear, look carefully—if he's over seventy he's probably not a hippily dressed grandfather but a Chelsea Pensioner out for a stroll. He'll probably know the way though as he's a local!

Remember that London Transport will gladly give a free bus or Underground map at one of their central stations—you can soon find your way about with the aid of these.

Where to Go and When

Carnaby Street

Carnaby Street runs parallel with Regent Street and is less than half a mile from the traditional men's tailoring area of Savile Row. The larger multiple stores in Oxford Street are also close at hand. Narrow Carnaby Street, however, has a heart of its own, which beats excitement and welcome to all. Although you can walk from one end to the other in three minutes, the fascination of the area could hold you for more than an hour. The most convenient tube station is Oxford Circus.

It may be useful to note that there are public conveniences at the junction of Great Marlborough Street, and that late closing for most shops in this area is on Thursday at about 7.30 p.m.

The Carnaby Street boutiques are listed in numerical order with the boutiques in neighbouring streets at the end of the section. If you wish to make a tour of them all it's best to follow the map on page 28, as you will note, the numbering in Carnaby Street goes down one side and up on the other, with the neighbouring boutiques scattered along its length.

Like the King's Road, the street is very lively on Saturdays. But go any time—you'll find a lot of people about and there's always something interesting happening.

The Village Store

5–7 Carnaby Street. *Girls.* Open Mon–Sat 9 am–6.30 pm. Thurs open until 7.30 pm. Barclaycard/American Express/Diners Club.

A John Stephen shop, strictly for birds. Some of the gear is more exclusive than you'll find at TRECAMP on page 42.

Dresses cost from about four pounds; coats from about eight pounds. There are coney furs for thirty-four pounds and fun-furs for only fifteen. Also a wide variety of hats and accessories.

One gets a startling glimpse here of just how prolific Mr. Stephen is.

Topper

9 Carnaby Street. *Girls and Men.* Open Mon–Sat 9 am–6 pm. Thurs and Fri open until 7 pm. Diners Club.

This boutique has a beautifully cool interior in weird purply shades. As well as men's shoes, Steve Topper has here a wide and original range of shoes for switched-on girls—all designed by himself and made up exclusively on the continent.

Prices for girls' shoes range from three pounds to five-pounds-fifteen; for boots, from five pounds—or ninety-nine-and-elevenpence! —to seven pounds-nineteen-and-six.

For more about men's shoes, see the other TOPPER shop at 45 Carnaby Street.

Donis

23–24 Carnaby Street. *Men.* Open
Mon–Sat 9 am–6 pm. Thurs open
until 7 pm. Barclaycard.

Andreas Spyropoulos came to Carnaby Street
soon after John Stephen in 1957. He has two
shops in the street and a third in Foubert's
Place. All three shops are called DONIS.

There are the usual accessories. Denim hipsters in all colours from sixty-five shillings.
Mohair trousers from seventy-five shillings.
Cord caps in every colour conceivable for a
guinea. Also, an interesting range of swimming
briefs priced from thirty-five shillings up to
fifty shillings.

Customers here have included a lot of stage
and screen personalities.

Mates

25 Carnaby Street. *Men and Girls.*
Open Mon–Sat 9 am–6.30 pm.
Thurs open until 7.30 pm.
Barclaycard/American Express/
Diners Club.

Details of the men's clothes kept at this Irvine
Sellars boutique can be found under TOMCAT
on page 36. The girls' clothes are downstairs:
Rings, belts, caps, berets, wigs, trouser suits,
dresses and coats. Dresses start at around two
pounds and there are versatile coat dresses for
four pounds-nine-and-six. How about a ravish-
ing suede trouser suit for twenty-eight guineas,
or a 'fun-fur' for thirty-six guineas?

Irvine Sellars

27 Carnaby Street. *Men.* Open
Mon–Sat 9 am–6.30 pm. Thurs
open until 7.30 pm. Barclaycard/
American Express/Diners Club.

For details of Irvine Sellars' stock, see below
under TOMCAT.

Tomcat

28 Carnaby Street. *Men.* Open
Mon–Sat 9 am–6.30 pm. Thurs
open until 7.30 pm. Barclaycard/
American Express/Diners Club.

TOMCAT is one of three shops owned by
Irvine Sellars. The others are called IRVINE
SELLARS and MATES, the latter having a girls'
section in the basement (see page 35).

The atmosphere here is lively and the clothes
are well displayed, just a few carefully selected
items being shown on the ground floor. You
may be attracted by a purple velvet suit for
twenty-five guineas, because of the way it
looks against a wall of deep magenta.

Downstairs is the main stock; ties, shirts,
jackets, trousers, capes and overcoats. Suits
cost from fifteen pounds off-the-peg, and from
thirty guineas to order. Capes with velvet
collars cost five pounds-fifteen. Leather overcoats cost from twenty-four guineas.

The designer is Liz Cloves and some of her
variations on current trends are really worth
looking out for. She got quite a lot of publicity
recently when she showed a version of a
Chinese Red Guard uniform. Last September
she had women's double-breasted pin stripe
trouser suits with turn-ups, almost identical
with those shown in January by Yves St.
Laurent.

Lady Jane

29 Carnaby Street. *Girls.* Open Mon–Sat 9.30 am–6.30 pm. Thurs open until 7.30 pm. Barclaycard/American Express/Diners Club.

LADY JANE caused a sensation when it opened last year. Two models were hired for three hours to change continuously in and out of the gear *in the shop window.* Nothing like that now, although one sees a lot of very pretty girls who must find quite a lot here to please them.

There are no accessories, but just about everything else you might want. Dresses cost from three pounds, spring coats from nine guineas, suits and trouser suits thirteen-and-a-half guineas. They also have quite a wide selection of furs, from twenty-six guineas.

Gear

35 Carnaby Street. *Everyone— including children.* Open Mon–Fri 9.30 am–6 pm. Sat close 4 pm.

Inviting looking place this. It's very hard just to pass by without looking in. Everything is pink and warm looking. The walls are all deep pink. Near the window there are thousands of bright feather flowers stuck in hundreds of pink tin tea-pots. There are also a lot of mobiles made with pink and orange wax discs.

GEAR started by selling furniture, and still have some rather nice old pine dressers which cost from twenty to fifty pounds. Now, however, they make up super children's clothes and sell everything from old coffee grinders (about four pounds ten), and Beardsley prints, to lapel

buttons that say corny things like 'I HATE
EVERYBODY'. They sell trays, plates, aprons,
carrier bags, teacloths and wastepaper baskets,
all decorated with the Union Jack. They even
have—Surprise! surprise!—flags decorated
with the Union Jack!

Other attractions include a free juke box and
a 'What-the-butler-saw' machine.

Male W.1.

38 Carnaby Street. *Men.* Open
Mon–Sat 9 am–6.30 pm. Thurs
open until 7.30 pm. Barclaycard/
American Express/Diners Club.

MALE W.1. is one of the smaller John Stephen
boutiques. One gets the feeling of walking into
a little side-show on a fairground. This
impression is strengthened by the music that
blares through the open doorway.

A full range is kept here of shirts, jackets,
trousers, ties and accessories, but only in small
quantities because of the size of the shop. For
fuller details of John Stephen clothes, see page
47 under JOHN STEPHEN.

Paul's Male Boutique

39 Carnaby Street. *Men.* Open
9 am–6.30 pm. Thurs open until
7.30 pm. Barclaycard/Diners Club.

This is the larger of two PAUL MALE
BOUTIQUES in the street. Both are owned by
Mr. Nat Spiegal, and both offer typical Carnaby
Street gear at typical local prices.

Stock includes all the common accessories.
Ties are wide or narrow, pointed or otherwise
according to the current trend. Shirts are priced

from around thirty shillings up to four-pounds-ten; trousers from four pounds. Two-piece suits 'off-the-peg' are priced from eleven pounds up to twenty.

His Clothes

41 Carnaby Street. *Men.* Open
9 am–6.30 pm. Thurs open until
7.30 pm. Barclaycard/American
Express/Diners Club.

This was the very first shop John Stephen opened in the street ten years ago. A lot of money has flowed through the cash register since then, but the shop hasn't wilted under the strain.

For information about the clothes, see page 47 under JOHN STEPHEN.

Lord John

43 Carnaby Street. *Men.* Open
9 am–6 pm. Thurs open until 7 pm.
Diners Club.

This is one of two shops owned by Mr. Warren Gold. For details of the stock, see under CARNABY HALL on page 50.

Topper

45 Carnaby Street. *Men.* Open
Mon–Sat 9 am–6 pm. Thurs and Fri
open until 7 pm. Diners Club.

Steve Topper, whose father ran a shoe business in Shaftesbury Avenue, has two shoe boutiques

in Carnaby Street, the other being for men and girls. He designs his collections of shoes and boots himself and has them made up in France and Italy. They are, in fact, very well made for the prices—between three pounds and ten guineas—and complement perfectly the clothes in the street.

Recent enthusiasts include the French singer, Johnny Halliday, who bought a pair of shoes in navy blue and white leather; the Small Faces, who chose suede casuals in bright green and plum; and Jimmy Tarbuck, who had a street version of a bowling shoe in beige suede and leather.

Steve Topper is convinced that the best way to assess people's personalities is to study their shoes, and, bearing this in mind, there should be food for thought in the above list.

Trecamp

46 Carnaby Street. *Girls.* Open 9 am–6.30 pm. Thurs open until 7.30 pm. Barclaycard/American Express/Diners Club.

John Stephen opened TRECAMP, the first girls' boutique in Carnaby Street, in the autumn of 1965. It is very small and intimate, tunnel-shaped, with a looking-glass covering the wall at the far end to give an impression of length. Girls may find it difficult to ignore the blown-up photographs of muscular young men in swimming trunks with which the fitting rooms are papered!!

Surprisingly enough, John Stephen offers as great a variety for girls as for boys. There are slacks, skirts, dresses, trouser suits, PVC macs, handbags and other accessories, with nothing terribly expensive. Sizes stocked range from 7's to 13's.

Domino Male

46a Carnaby Street. *Men.* Open
Mon–Sat 9 am–6.30 pm. Thurs
open until 7.30 pm. Barclaycard/
American Express/Diners Club

Yet another John Stephen shop, next door to
TRECAMP and tied in with it by a delicately
drawn classical façade.

A little of everything is kept here, but because
of the extreme lack of space, no big stocks.
Again, it's what one might call intimate. For
information about John Stephen clothes, see
page 47 under JOHN STEPHEN.

Paul's Male Boutique

47 Carnaby Street. *Men.* Open
Mon–Sat 9 am–6 pm. Thurs open
until 7 pm. Diners Club.

This is a smaller version of the PAUL'S MALE
BOUTIQUE at No. 39.

See page 39 for further information.

Adam W.1

47a Carnaby Street. *Men.* Open
Mon–Sat 9 am–6 pm. Thurs open
until 7 pm. Barclaycard/American
Express/Diners Club.

This is a very small boutique with not much

room to breathe. The clothes are all typical Carnaby Street stuff. Shirts at around thirty-five shillings, trousers at seventy shillings.

A larger version of Adam W.1 commands a prominent position on the corner of Foubert's Place and Kingly Street with a good range of stock.

John Stephen's
Man's Shop

49 Carnaby Street. *Men.*
Open Mon–Sat 9 am–6.30 pm.
Thurs open until 7.30 pm.
Barclaycard/American Express
Diners Club.

At last, a shop you can breathe in! Quite a large stock is kept here and, for once, the windows are not overcrowded. In fact, the window displays are very 'with-it' and usually very eye-catching.

John Stephen boutiques give you the feeling that nothing is left to chance and that everything has been done to attract and service would be visitors.

As well as the full range of John Stephen 'ready-to-wear' clothes, a tailored suit can also be ordered. No bulky rolls of material blocking out the light as in a traditional tailor's, but books of neat samples—and strictly first-class cloths.

A two-piece suit here will cost anything from thirty to sixty guineas. It can be classical and unassertive, or as crazy as you like. Ian or Giorgio will look after you, and give you what you want as though that was all they lived for. According to Ian, 'you have to dress the mind as well as the figure'—which means understanding the client's idea of himself.

Service is excellent. Delivery takes between three and four weeks, and fittings are always on time. No delays, except on the very rare occasions when the supply of an unusual particular material is held up.

John Stephen

52–55 Carnaby Street. *Men and Girls* Open Mon–Sat 9 am–6.30 pm. Thurs open until 7.30 pm. Barclaycard/American Express/ Diners Club.

The main JOHN STEPHEN shop, catering for both girls and boys. It is spacious, by Carnaby Street standards, and the music is kept at a pleasant volume.

Men's wear at all the JOHN STEPHEN shops is within a medium price range. Shirts cost between forty-nine and elevenpence and four guineas; trousers between fifty-nine and elevenpence and six guineas; off-the-peg suits between twelve and twenty-five guineas.

JOHN STEPHEN also does a range of cosmetics for men, including cologne at thirty-five shillings, pre-shave and after-shave lotions, each at twenty-nine and sixpence, and talcum powder at nineteen and sixpence.

The clientele includes all the usual pop personalities, and you may see such celebrities as Lord Snowdon, the Duke of Bedford and Peter Sellers.

Foale and Tuffin

1 Marlborough Court. *Girls.* Open Mon–Fri 10 am–6 pm. Thurs open until 7 pm. Sat open until 3 pm.

All the clothes here are designed by Marion Foale and Sally Tuffin, and the standard is way above what may be called 'standard Carnaby Street'.

Everything is very original and well finished. Colour is an important factor and is usually strong enough to make an impact despite the red, white and blue interior of the shop. Prices, however, are quite high. Dresses cost from eight guineas, suits and trouser suits from about twenty guineas, coats from sixteen guineas. There are also exclusive handbags that average about four-and-a-half guineas.

Altogether, you won't be surprised that most of the celebrities who come here—people like Cathy McGowan and Francoise Hardy—come again and again. It is also notable that the products here are spoken of with respect by the art school crowd, a discerning 'with-it' group.

The Button Queen

5 Marlborough Court. *Men and Girls.* Open Mon–Wed 10 am–5 pm. Thurs and Fri 10 am–6 pm. Closed Sat.

Toni Frith came to Carnaby Street from the Portobello Road in 1962. She originally started dealing in buttons because she hadn't a car and —'buttons are nice and portable'. Now they are her life. She's interested in the whole ethos of the period from which a button comes and does research once a week at the Victoria and Albert Museum.

Her old and antique buttons can be used as buttons or made up into ear-rings or unusual cuff links which are certainly smarter than the more mass-produced products in Carnaby Street.

Carnaby Hall

27–28 Gt. Marlborough Street.
Men. Open 9 am–6 pm. Thurs open until 7 pm. Barclaycard/Diners Club

This is one of two shops owned by Mr. Warren Gold, the other being LORD JOHN at 43 Carnaby Street. Neither shop has anything to do with John Stephen.

The quality at both shops is pretty much what you might call 'average Carnaby Street' and so are the prices. There's a wide range of accessories, shirts, trousers, jackets and knitwear—all reflecting the latest trends and not exactly built to last for a lifetime. A ready-to-wear suit costs from round twelve pounds and upward, while one made to measure costs from eighteen guineas.

Take Six

34 Gt. Marlborough Street.
Men. Open 9 am–6 pm. Thurs open until 7 pm. Barclaycard/Diners Club.

About six years ago designer, Sydney Brent, made a suit all in paisley. This was a joke, but it sold the very first day that it was shown and there were many orders for more like it. So, thought Mr. Brent, 'What the hell. . . .' Apparently, anything new goes!

Well, he's obviously kept busy having new ideas at 'Take Six', a branch of the Brent and Collins Group—other branches in Essex. He designed the Troggs' first outfits, and gear for many other Groups.

The prices are competitive—too competitive for some shop owners, according to a recent article in *The Outfitter*. An off-the-peg suit costs from something like nine guineas—in mohair from fourteen guineas—and you can have a suit made to measure for as little as eighteen guineas.

All the usual accessories are here, as well as shirts, trousers, top coats and capes. A rather nice speciality is a coachman jacket made to order in suede.

Vince

15 Newburgh Street. *Men.* Open Mon–Fri 9 am–6 pm. Thurs open until 7.30 pm. Sat close 4 pm.

This was the very first men's boutique around Carnaby Street. The temptation to mass-produce has been resisted; everything is exclusive and designed by Vince Green himself.

The speciality here is still swimming briefs, mostly made in stretch materials and costing from seventeen-and-sixpence to fifty shillings. Trousers are made in a variety of materials, including denim and stretch cloths for between three and eight guineas. Mohair trousers cost five guineas. Shirts range from thirty-five shillings to seven guineas. There are also quite a lot of nice caps and a few ties in unusual designs.

The clientele is distinguished—Keep your eyes open.

Hat Gear

12 Ganton Street. *Men and Girls.*
Open Mon–Sat 9 am–6 pm.
Thurs open until 8 pm.

This is one of the aristocrats among shops in the Carnaby Street district. The decor is entirely congruous with the dignified eighteenth century house in which it is set. Colour and fantasy are supplied by the hats, which tend to range in price from thirty-five shillings to one hundred and five guineas. Model hats and 'mod' hats, wonderful great floppy hats, sailor caps, toreador hats, silk, straw, velvet, beaver, corduroy, sealskin, mink, cotton . . . in all colours and in jet black.

George Mallard has been making and designing model hats in Ganton Street for fourteen years. Started with 'gear' hats four years ago to meet a growing demand led by Nureyev, Sophia Loren, Lena Horne, Elke Somner, Rita Tushingham, Herman of the Hermits, and many others. Opened a workroom in the East End to help cope with the demand.

However different, none of George Mallard's hats is a 'joke hat'. Whether hand-stitched or machined, each one is made to be worn and admired.

Palisades

26 Ganton Street. *Girls.* Open Mon–Fri 10 am–6 pm. Thurs open until 7 pm. Sat open until 2 pm.

PALISADES is another boutique that stands somewhat apart from Carnaby Street, both in fact and in spirit. The decor is simple and you don't have to shout because there isn't any music—just the sweet sound of film stars and models gasping with admiration.

Pauline Fordham, who runs the shop, is interested in revival. She follows her own inclinations, however. You'll find beautiful versions of the 15th century smock shirt for five-and-a-half guineas. Anything, however eccentric, can be made up to order from about twenty guineas for a dress.

Dresses in stock usually start from around four guineas; coats from eight guineas. There are also some gloves, belts, watch straps and other accessories.

I Was Lord Kitchener's Valet

15 Foubert's Place. *Men and Girls* Open Mon.–Sat. 9.30 a.m. to 6 p.m. Thurs. open until 7 p.m.

Well worth a visit. This boutique specialises in the sale of period military uniforms. The assistants at the boutique are also dressed in period costume. The atmosphere, however, is nothing like the Quartermaster's stores. Military marches and not beat is the musical backing. Capes £2.10.0 to £5.10.0; tunics £3.10.0 to £12.10.0. Some capes are up to 60 years old. Another branch at 293 Portobello Road.

Gear Goes for a Stroll

Olé

King's Road

The boutiques are spread fairly evenly along the King's Road for something like a mile and a quarter. The effect of the gear scene is therefore not as concentrated as it is in Carnaby Street.

If you want the full effect come here on a Saturday, when the pavements and the shops are packed with gear people. The restaurants and pubs will also be doing a roaring trade. If you want to see the effect of the fashion revolution at a swift glance, drop in to a pub on the South side of the road called the 'Chelsea Potter' or take a look in 'Finch's' or the 'Six Bells'—all in the main road.

If you simply want to buy clothes on the other hand, you'll find it easier if you can come in a weekday. Remember that Thursday is early closing. Low street numbers commence at Sloane Square end. Odd numbers are on the left and even numbers on the right. Other boutiques in the area are at the end of the section. For location of boutiques follow the map on page 30.

Sidney Smith Man's Shop

36 King's Road. *Men.* Open
Mon–Sat 9 am–6 pm. Thurs close
at 1 pm. Fri open until 7 pm.

Jonathan Smith opened the first SIDNEY
SMITH MAN'S SHOP three years ago but the
firm of Sidney Smith has been in the King's
Road for sixty years. Having solid foundations
does have its advantages: Sidney Smith have
built up a lot of good will and get really good
service from their manufacturers.

It's Jonathan Smith's belief that fewer
people now are prepared to pay simply for
design. They want bright, modern clothes that
can be worn and washed or cleaned—and
want them at reasonable prices. There's good
service and a comprehensive range of accessories, ties, shirts, trousers, coats and military
capes that certainly give value for money.
Average price for an off-the-peg suit is about
nineteen guineas.

This isn't the most startling shop in the King's
Road but it would have startled—and possibly
delighted—the firm's founder.

Fifth Avenue

84 King's Road. *Men.* Open
Mon–Sat 9 am–6 pm. Thurs close
at 1 pm. Fri open until 7 pm.

In opening a fifth gear boutique in the King's
Road, FIFTH AVENUE of Regent Street and
Oxford Street have suitably and stunningly
switched from traditional clothing to really

with-it fashions. The brilliantly coloured clothes and accessories are shown off against austere black and white backgrounds in an interior made to look like a system of grottoes. For further atmosphere there are modern sculptures and pop music.

If you feel out of place in this sort of atmosphere there's everything you need to get you in the mood quickly. The stock is enormous —and much of it exclusive. Prices range from six or seven shillings for costume jewellery to 500 guineas for a fur coat.

John Stephen

97 King's Road. *Men.* Open Mon–Sat 9 am–6 pm. Thurs close 1 pm. Fri open until 7 pm. Diners Club/American Express.

This is the main John Stephen store in the King's Road and the tone is very different from that to be found in Carnaby Street. It's all coach lamps, brass and quality.

A good selection of everything can be found here—the usual accessories, slick watches, shirts, trousers, plus whatever happens to be the current rage in North West Soho.

It should be borne in mind that, except for a few 'classic' or best-selling lines, you won't find the same shirt in any two J.S. shops. Prices, of course, are not too high and the quality is what one has come to expect. More details of the JOHN STEPHEN range are in the Carnaby Street list.

John Michael

106 King's Road. *Men.* Open
Mon–Sat 9 am–6 pm. Thurs close
1 pm. Barclaycard/American
Express.

As usual with JOHN MICHAEL shops, this is a
very discreet place. There's no music. The
decor is simple with a whole lot of white painted
wood. The suggestion is one of quality and
taste.

Prices, too, are rather quality ones but there's
no danger of the products falling to pieces after
a few days. The designs are all very elegant and
discreet. Shirts cost from four guineas, suits
from thirty two guineas. A suit made to measure
costs from about fifty five guineas.

For the man who wants to look modern but
not too way out, this is a very good place to
shop. The first Beatle suit was made by John
Michael—and what better guarantee can there
be than that ?

Michael's Man Boutique

122 King's Road. *Men.* Open
Mon–Sat 9.30 am–6 pm. Thurs
close 1 pm. Barclaycard/American
Express/Diners Club.

No connection here between this shop and
John Michael. What's more they say so
explicitly with a notice in the window and
implicitly by a cheerful hard edge mural on the
left as you walk in. The mural, by David Cripps
contrasts with a general decor of grey brick
white painted wood and a stark black stairway.

Over the stairs is a sort of inverted New York skyline in polystyrene commissioned from David Bartlett.

There are, of course, clothes too. A comprehensive range and, because Michael's have been manufacturing for a long time, the prices are very reasonable. There is a particularly stunning selection of sweaters, many of them made up exclusively to Michael's designs— from 4 guineas upward. Exclusive tailoring is offered from about 25 guineas for jacket and trousers and, for a moderate price you can kit yourself out for a Chinese funeral or any other unusual event you fancy.

Top Gear and Countdown

135a–137 King's Road. *Girls.*
Open Mon–Sat 10 am–8 pm.
Thurs close 1 pm.

Here are two very exciting shops and you'll be struck at once by the beautiful clothes and accessories and by the decor. The interior of COUNTDOWN is in polished silver metal. This gives a really super-modern effect and emphasises the femininity of the clothes. Also of the beautiful girls—you won't have seen so many in so small a space ever before. Girls who want their men to take them shopping here may like to point this out.

The designer is James Wedge—and he's a designer who integrates design and colour superbly. A dress costs from 3 to 9 pounds, knitted dresses from 8 to 10 guineas trouser suits from 15 to 21 pounds. It's worth noting that small sizes are stocked, right down to size six.

Of the two shops COUNTDOWN is slightly the more splendid and slightly more expensive. Shopping here is really enjoyable. They will send you a mail order catalogue for 2 shillings if you can't make that particular scene.

Bazaar

138 King's Road. *Girls.* Next door to the 'Markham Arms'. Open Mon–Sat 9.30 am–5.30 pm. Thurs close 1 pm.

Although Mary Quant disapproves of the word 'boutique' and the whole BAZAAR outfit is now strictly professional, there's no loss of excitement in the shop that started it all. The stock inside changes as often as the window displays and there are constantly new ideas from such bright young designers as Harvey Gould, Gerald McCann, Jean Muir, Roger Nelson, Jan Stevens and James Wedge—as well as from Mary Quant herself.

No one presses you to buy here but the service when you want it, is patient and prompt. The music is relaxing and the prices are nothing to get upset about. Cosmetics are from 7/6d., dresses from about 5 pounds, furs from 75 guineas.

Other branches of BAZAAR are at 46 Brompton Road S.W.3, and at 113 New Bond Street, W.1.

Dandie Fashions

161 King's Road. *Men.* Open Mon–Sat 11 am–6.30 pm.

When DANDIE FASHIONS first opened the Rolling Stones bought the entire stock. The place is constantly full of similarly discriminating gentlemen (and you might see Brigitte Bardot—if you're lucky!).

Outside, rainbow painting contrasts strikingly with large gloomy windows. A more than life-size bust of Apollo stares bleakly out. Inside, more rainbow painting contrasts with stuffed birds. The mixture is somewhere between a lumber room in an old English house and a psychedelic freak out party.

DANDIE FASHIONS, opened originally by John Crittel in Gloucester Mews, moved to the King's Road this February. There's a lot of very handsome revivalist stuff—velvet Georgian topcoats for instance. Suits can be made to measure for 32 guineas upward; shoes made to measure for 6 guineas upward; trousers also from 6 guineas. There's a wide range of unusual ready-made gear that includes ties by Niko Kerman and exclusive silk screened shirts.

Guy

170 King's Road. *Men.* Opposite the 'Chelsea Potter'. Open Mon–Sat 9 am–6 pm. Thurs close 1 pm.

This is a smaller version of the other GUY shops in the West End, including Nos. 259 and 388 Oxford Street. Fewer of the more conservative lines will be found here, however, and you're more likely to see daring exploits of the commercial shirt-maker that won't be seen in Oxford Street. Stock includes a little of everything—accessories, ties, trousers, shirts (from about two pounds), knitwear, suits (from eighteen guineas), and top coats. Because of the lack of space, the stock is not enormous.

GUY shops belong to, and are a less expensive version of JOHN MICHAEL.

His Clothes

201 King's Road. *Men.* Open
Mon–Sat 9 am–6 pm. Thurs close
1 pm. Fri open until 7 pm.
American Express/Diners Club.

A John Stephen shop, smaller than No. 97.
No suits or coats but a wide selection of casual
wear, shirts and sweaters. Also ties and the
usual accessories.

Chelsea Antique Market

253 King's Road. *Men and Girls.*
Opposite Carlyle Square. Open
Mon 10 am–1 pm. Tues–Sat
10 am–6 pm.

On the first and second floor of the CHELSEA
ANTIQUE MARKET, Messrs. Emmerton and
Lambert sell a fascinating assortment of old
clothes. There are Victorian knickers, nightshirts,
gangster hats, topees—'anything that's a
giggle'. A lot of it, however, is very very wear-
able. What about a lovely organza boa for 45
shillings, or some really good 120's cravats
(Liberty prints) for 12/6d.?
   This is a place worth visiting regularly.
Unusual things keep turning up and they
usually go pretty quickly. One's likely to
become addicted, anyway.

Simon Shop

341 King's Road. *Men and Girls.*
Open Mon–Sat 10 am–6 pm. Thurs
close at 1 pm. Fri open until 7 pm.

A rare shop, this—very modern—but with something of what the eighteenth century Regency snobs called 'ton'. A copper plate in the window announces that a Savile Row tailor is in attendance, and he really is. All the time. He's to be seen—in braces and trousers up to his chest and all—looking very inscrutable as he gives fittings to groups like 'the Move'.

Actually, Mr. Brindle is a champion of the gear scene. The suits he makes are some of the best combinations you see of craftsmanship and bold design—very high waisted with box pleats; just the sort of stuff Pierre Cardin tries to imitate. They cost from 24 pounds off the peg, and from 45 pounds made to measure. For summer evening wear, he has Levi-type jackets in Duchess satin and velvet—costing from about 10 guineas.

For girls, dresses start at about 4 guineas—in pure silk from 25 guineas. Furs are made to order from about 35 guineas.

All designs are by either Simon Boyle or Peter Young, and are as original as any in London.

Gloryhole Boutique

342 King's Road. *Mostly Girls.*
Opposite Pautton's Square. Open
Mon–Sat 10.30 am–6 pm.
Fri open until 7 pm.

This was originally a girl's shop, but some very good men's things are now sold here, too. Mixed shopping is pleasant in the intimate setting of a small boutique particularly when there's music, as there is here. It's nice to have the chance to tread on the toes of the likes of Dusty Springfield or Pattie Boyd.

The stock is almost all designed by Gerald McCann.

Susan Locke

414 King's Road. *Mostly Girls.*
Open Mon–Sat 10 am–6.30 pm.
Fri open until 7 pm.

If you're coming straight here from the Sloane Square end of the King's Road, take a bus or a taxi. Arrive, anyway, in a mood to be receptive. This is a boutique even other boutique owners say you mustn't miss!

Susan Locke herself designs new clothes every week. They're original and well made. Dresses cost from around 3 pounds, and all sizes from 7 to 15 are usually in stock. Also there are the usual accessories and, in fact, everything except underwear and coats. Boots and shoes are made to order by Terry de Havilland. For men, there are very pretty cuff links and ties.

4.30

430 King's Road. *Mostly Girls.*
Open Mon–Sat 10.30 am–6.30 pm.
Thurs close at 1 pm. Fri open
until 8 pm.

Carol Derry, who runs this shop, is a very charming young woman. What's more, her prices must be the lowest in the King's Road. Summer skirts cost from 25 shillings to 2 pounds. Dresses from thirty-nine-and-eleven-pence to seventy shillings. Trouser suits average from eight pounds to eight-pounds-ten.

Carol Derry makes up everything in 4.30 herself—and it's all beautifully finished. In addition to what has already been mentioned, there are quite a lot of accessories, including some very original and exclusive handbags. You can get a splendid evening bag in silver suede with shiny metal discs for only three-pounds-ten. There are also a good range of trendy belts for men.

Granny Takes a Trip

488 King's Road. *Men and Girls.*
Open Mon–Sat 10 am–7 pm.
Thurs close at 1 pm.

This is just about the end of the road. The exterior defies description, but the interior is probably supposed to be 'a la Beardsley', to judge from the prominently placed book of his drawings. The walls and ceiling are purple. There's a green, tasselled light shade, a phonograph, a Victorian looking glass, and a black silk Victorian sun shade. Beardsley might not have liked it, but it's great fun. Like a not-too-expensive Victorian brothel might have looked.

GRANNY TAKES A TRIP no longer sell second-hand stuff, but most of what they have has the 'period' flavour. Men's trousers cost 6 guineas; shirts from 4 to 10 guineas; jackets from 15 guineas; blouses from 4 to 7 guineas. They have some high-necked lace Victorian blouses for $6\frac{1}{2}$ guineas; summery Indian print dresses for $6\frac{1}{2}$ guineas.

Just Men

9 Tryon Street. *Men.* Open
Mon–Sat 9.30 am–7 pm.
Thurs close at 1 pm.

Tryon Street is the fifth turning off the King's
Road from the Sloane Square end. The boutique
is just about fifty yards down on the left—and it
should, on no account, be overlooked.

Even without the stimulating music and the
decor, the clothes would knock you out. There
are fabulous suede and leather suits, flared
trousers, tapering shirts and the most brilliant
display of way-out ties and accessories.

Prices are pretty reasonable for this kind of
gear. Shirts cost from three pounds; trousers
from five pounds. Trousers can be made to your
own exclusive design for eight pounds, and
they're amongst the best trousers in London.
Suits made to measure can cost anything from
thirty pounds.

The Shop

47 Radnor Walk. *Girls.* Open
Mon-Fri 10 am – 7 pm.
Thurs close 1 pm.

From Sloane Square, Radnor Walk is on the
left-hand side of the road, before 135a King's
Road. The shop has been there for 2½ years.
All the clothes are designed by Maurice Jeffrey
and are made on the premises. Trouser suits
(all fully lined), including skirts, range from
six pounds ten shillings up to ten guineas.
Floral coats, of varying lengths, cost about
seven guineas. Light fabric dresses cost as
little as two pounds ten shillings up to three
pounds ten shillings.

Things To Come

Gear designers and beat groups are often asked in interviews on radio, television and in the press what the future of the scene holds for us. They never really know. The gear scene is a rapidly changing one. The boutiques seem to grow overnight sometimes. Fashion is not dictated by any one thing. The changing nature of the trends have led some observers to say that the scene is a passing one. This seems unlikely. What is difficult is to be able to forecast what will be in-wear in a few months' time. At the time of writing there is a big demand and liking for old uniforms and military gear, for Victoriana and for wearing plastic and PVC gear in bright colours and rather futuristic designs.

Fashion seems to be dictated by a variety of factors. The pop groups have a big influence. The leading with-it fashion designers constantly come up with new way-out ideas. No one can know what will be next—that's half the fun. You will hear all sorts of ideas bandied about. Draw your own conclusions. The idea of 'functionalism' is strong at the moment—for simplified designs dictated partly by mass production, using materials that are spongeable or disposable, for example simple paper dresses for girls. You can now buy paper dresses that are quite fireproof in with-it styles and prices are coming down fast—at the moment you may find them for less than a pound each. The boutiques are on to paper shoes to match.

There are even plain paper dresses which you colour to your own designs—a clever idea for the amateur designer. It's quite likely that soon you'll be able to get a couple of mini-dresses and a pair of shoes, all in paper, and still have change from a pound note. 'Revival' is another line. It may be reviving one period or another, depending on the mood of the designers and customers. Lacy Victorian dresses modified to the latest lengths are popular but so are the Edwardian coats and ruffles for men—both the real thing in the second-hand boutiques and new imitations with modifications in the others.

Dizzy Days

There certainly seems to be a moving together of the sexes in some of the gear worn. Male hair styles are often long and dandy, female ones may be very short and rather masculine. Many of the girls have taken to wearing men's gear while the men are wearing what would, ten years ago, be regarded as feminine looking trends. There has been quite a lot of nonsense talked by sociologists and interpreters of the scene about the significance of these changes and reversals. Most of it is meaningless. What is true is that all sorts of styles go. If it looks good, then let's do it—is the governing feeling. Decoration has always been part of dress. In some periods it has been restrained—often by religious movements. And yet even here it is hard to draw hard and fast lines. The Victorian era was said to be a strictly puritan one yet leaders like Disraeli happily appeared in the House of Commons wearing velvet coats, colourful cravats and white gloves with rings on the outside of the fingers!

The pendulum of fashion has always seemed to swing to and fro—it's just swinging at the moment! A period of gay and lively dress for male or female would usually be followed by a more sober era. Wartime, of course, invariably causes dress to become dull and quiet. There are more important things to think about and materials are scarce. Thus the First World War was a drab period followed by the 'flapper' age of the twenties. The Second World War was again a time when dress was anything but elegant. It took us some time to snap out of the rather dreary wear of the forties and early fifties. Now, however, with young people taking the lead in dress and with a large number of people able and willing to spend money on their looks, there seems no reason why we should not go on to even greater things. It's certain that not even Mary Quant or John Michael could tell you what will be the trend in five years' time. It will probably be a mixture of the use of old fashions from other ages and very modern materials. New plastics and man-made fibres now give the designers ideas and opportunities they have never had before. If men start travelling in space —and it certainly looks as though they will— then we are bound to see gear for the space age taking a more important part in the scene. Gaily coloured plastic suits with zips or maybe simple fastenings which use two different plastics to hold them together will be the sort of gear at one end of the scene—more and more exotic ideas from the past, using new materials but old designs, may well be another field. There have been dresses made entirely out of aluminium discs or plastic buttons which clink sexily as you walk along. Designers have even come up with gear made out of sheets of light metal—pretty uncomfortable but really space age looking. Another idea is the transparent plastic dress with body decoration showing through it. These new ideas have produced completely new fashions. The shortness of the mini-skirt produced tights for girls and even long coloured pants which show below the hemline. Now the stocking manufacturers have come out with self-supporting tops, so there's no chance of suspenders showing when you sit down—'the last of the great suspenders' as one firm calls it.

Not Only Fashion

Remember when in the Carnaby Street or King's Road areas—or any part of London with a fashion scene—to keep your eyes open for the rest of the scene. Clothes are one aspect of it, but London is now full of other interesting shops and places which all form part of the same movement. Fashion overflows from the gear to wear to gear for living. Take a look in some of the furniture boutiques and the modern bookshops. There are some of these in both areas. Designers have taken up the way-out ideas for re-doing old furniture. You can see chests of drawers painted up in art nouveau patterns, or blazoned with Union Jacks. There are old grandfather clocks with swinging new designs on them, Victoriana adapted to match the gear people are wearing. You can buy furnishings and fabrics in mod designs which set off the new clothes and this extends upwards to bigger things like cars and downwards to stationery and knicknacks. Shops like TRAD in the Portobello Road, GEAR in Carnaby Street or DODO in Westbourne Grove all stock way-out bill posters, mad old Victorian household equipment, postcards and drawings which are a mixture of modern painting trends and antique gimmickry. Like the clothes, the accent tends to be on bright colours and new materials mixed with objects from former periods.

There are even groups of designers who will 'customize' your car. You may see one of these driving around Soho or Sloane Square—perhaps painted all over with stripes or art nouveau patterns. They form a part of the scene. Or walk into the with-it bookshops—DIDICA in Southampton Row or BETTER BOOKS in Charing Cross Road. Here you will find articles and books about the scene, gear people browsing or just talking.

If you just want to sample the scene you can't do better than some of the pubs. Try Heneky's in the Portobello Road—the big area for antiques which also has some boutiques around—Saturday lunchtime is the best time. You'll see a wonderful collection of gear being worn, military uniforms, very mini-skirts (almost pelmet skirts!), in fact anything that goes. Or drop in to any of the pubs on a Saturday in the Greek Street and Dean Street area of Soho, only about ten minutes' walk from Carnaby Street. For an outing, try taking the Underground to Hampstead and walk down the High Street—again Saturday is the best time. You'll get a glimpse of what the gear looks like in very pleasant surroundings and there are several good boutiques, antique shops and places selling with-it furniture and ornaments. Off the High Street are lots of little alleys. Walk up Perrin's Court and take a look in THAT NEW SHOP or along Flask Walk and have a drink in THE FLASK—full of novelists and gear dressed television types.

The scene is all around you but London is a big city and hides some of its offerings. People are always very willing to help you find what you want. Try going into the Institute of Contemporary Arts in Dover Street off Piccadilly. There will probably be a gang of gear looking people in there together with some very way-out exhibitions. There are plenty of posters to tell you about scene happenings and events. Quite often there's something on at the week-end at the ROUNDHOUSE right beside Chalk Farm Underground station—a psychedelic jumble sale or a showing of underground movies—a good place for seeing the scene. Whatever you find, you can be sure that there will be plenty happening on the London scene.